Appetizer Rex

By Kentaro Kobayashi

Photography by Hideo Sawai

VERTICAL.

Contents

Numbers in parentheses indicate recipe page

Appetizer Rex

Despite outward appearances, I'm not a heavy drinker. But when I do kick back with a beer, I want to have a nice dish to go along with it—no sad bowl of peanuts for me. I have the opportunity to drink with friends fairly often. I have people over to my place and people invite me out as well. There's always beer and wine (at the very least) served at these get-togethers, and I always like to have some delectable hors d'oeuvres to serve and enjoy.

The joy of preparing appretizers is slightly different from the pleasure of cooking a big meal. For appetizers, you make just what you want at that moment, and only cook as much as you need. It's not necessarily a balanced or filling meal, it's "food that's fun." That's the best part. You can make all your favorite dishes—greasy and good, hot and spicy, sour and refreshing, crunchy and toothsome—anything that you happen to crave. And setting out homemade food is always a thrill that you just can't get when using store-bought products.

A while back, I had one of those days at work and ended up getting home just 20 minutes before my friends were due to arrive. So I quickly chopped up some vegetable to make pickles and tossed them into the refrigerator. My friends arrived in no time, and I put the pickles on one of my favorite large serving dishes and set it on the table. Dishing out lots of food on big platters not only looks dynamic, it makes everything seem that much more appealing. Keep in mind that presentation is important. That's not just for big groups, you know. Treat yourself to the nice, big dishes, too.

First we all went for Rolling Rock, a beer I've liked ever since trying it in New York. Lightly pickled vegetables are a perfect complement for the light beer. Everyone loved the idea of a rare (for Japan) beer. After saying cheers I put some cheese crackers into the toaster oven, and in a flash the second dish was out. After cool, refreshing pickles, a warm, crispy rice cracker is just perfect. While dancing around a few questions on how to make the crackers, I started prepping the fried oysters. As everyone settled into their seats and the conversation grew lively, I brought out more beer and started to cook. As I enjoyed the privilege of minding the pan and the chatter at once, and as the first CD ended, the crispy, crunchy fried oysters were ready to be served. Served simply with salt, the oysters made the beer disappear even faster. When placed in front of a pair of hungry eyes, a plate of well-cooked fried oysters will vanish in a flash. Shouldn't food always be that tempting?

I brought the last of the pickles to the table and took a seat. We switched to wine and I sliced up some cheese, and we talked about silly things. Silly conversations go best with drinks. When the wine ran out, I brought out the rice dish finale. The bonito flakes, green onions and seaweed served over rice turned out to be another hit. Our conversations about nothing carried on long after we looked stupefied with contentment. By the time coffee was served and I saw everyone out the door, it was close to midnight.

Even on your busiest days, if you have a few minutes, a couple of tricks to make dishes quickly, a relaxed attitude, good music, silly topics of conversation and this book, you'll find out just how great it is to be the Appetizer Rex.

Quick Fix Dishes

You've invited a few friends over, but nothing's ready. You're exhausted after a long day, but you want a snack with your drink. For those times, try making these "quick fix" dishes. They're perfect in a pinch. Serve up something easy, have a nip of a cocktail, then dive into cooking the main course. If you're just cooking for one, enjoy these easy dishes while savoring your favorite wine. These recipes are satisfying without eating up all your time and energy.

Light Pickles
Like a light marinade

Most people think pickles need to be stored away for days before you can eat them, but this dish is refreshing, like a salad, rather than potently sour. If you have 15 minutes, you can whip up these light pickles. Of course, if you have the time and want the flavors to seep in, you can always prepare this a day in advance. Either way, these easy pickles are a smart dish that can be enjoyed whenever the craving strikes.

A light sprinkle of curry powder

Ingredients

1 head cauliflower
1 small red bell pepper
1 small yellow bell pepper
1 cucumber
1/2 onion
1 tsp salt

A ⎰ 2 Tbsp olive oil
3 Tbsp rice vinegar
1 tsp sugar
Pinch salt
Pepper, to taste
Curry powder, to taste
1 chili pepper, deseeded

Instructions

1. Break up cauliflower into smaller pieces and simmer in lightly salted water.
2. Dice bell peppers into 1" (2 to 3 cm) pieces. Slice cucumber into 1" rounds. Thinly slice onion.
3. Add vegetables to a bowl and sprinkle with salt, then stir lightly. Set aside for 2 to 3 minutes. Rinse.
4. Add mixture A to a separate bowl. Add vegetables and mix. Cover with plastic wrap and refrigerate for at least 15 minutes.

Tomato Salsa

The fresh fragrance will whet your appetite

A great, tasty condiment, whether it's a dip for chips or toast, or to top off grilled chicken or fish. An easy-to-make Mexican dish that'll get your tummy rumbling for more and leave your taste buds ready for a drink. This is a personal favorite of mine.

Cutting all vegetables to the same size is important

Ingredients

1 tomato
1/2 onion
1 stalk celery
Bunch celery leaves, finely chopped
2 Tbsp lemon juice
1/2 tsp salt
Pepper, to taste
Tabasco sauce, to taste

Instructions

1. Finely dice all vegetables.
2. Add all ingredients to a bowl and stir.

Note

Salsa means "sauce" in Spanish. Mexican salsa traditionally includes a chili pepper.

Nachos

Pile ingredients high, then bake

If you get bored with dishes that are just tossed together or simply marinated, try this grilled delight for a nice twist.

Add an accent with chili powder

Ingredients

Corn chips, to taste
Several stuffed green olives
2 to 3 Tbsp tomato sauce
Shredded mozzarella cheese, to taste
Chili powder, to taste
Pepper, to taste

Instructions

Add tortilla chips to an oven-safe dish. Cut olives in half and sprinkle over chips. Add remaining ingredients on top, then place in toaster oven (or oven) and broil.

Salmon Dip and Avocado Dip
Always great with drinks

With veggie sticks or on crackers, these dips are delicious. This is a dish that's handy anytime. Canned salmon comes out beautifully and the avocado is surprisingly light.

Use garlic with the canned salmon to remove fishy odor

Ingredients
1 can (6 1/2 oz (180 g)) salmon
3 1/2 Tbsp (50 g) cream cheese
Grated garlic, to taste
1 Tbsp mayonnaise
Pinch salt
Pepper, to taste

Instructions
Blend all ingredients together in a bowl.

Use a very ripe avocado

Ingredients
1 avocado, 1 Tbsp lemon juice, 1/8 onion,
3 1/2 Tbsp (50 g) cream cheese,
1 Tbsp mayonnaise, pinch salt

Instructions
1. Slice avocado in half and remove pit and skin. Combine avocado and lemon juice in a bowl.
2. Mince onion.
3. Add all ingredients to bowl with avocado and stir until smooth.

Note
Avocado oxidizes easily. They say if you keep the pit in the mixture the color will stay greener longer. I tried it out and it really seems to work.

Tomato and Olive Bruschetta

A simple and delicious dish

Bruschetta's flavor is a simple combination of oil, salt and garlic.
Don't try to make it over-complicated. Trust me, it'll be delicious.
This dish goes well with straight gin or vodka.

Spicy Pickled Cucumber

Nice and crunchy

Cut the cucumbers into big pieces. Heat the sauce in a pot, then mix into cucumbers, letting the flavors seep in. If you have time, let it cool so it can marinate even longer.

Adding heated sauce is the trick to make this dish in no time flat

Ingredients

2 to 3 cucumbers

1 tsp salt

A
- 2 Tbsp soy sauce
- 1/2 Tbsp sesame oil
- 1/2 Tbsp rice vinegar
- 1 Tbsp sake
- 3 red chili peppers

Instructions

1. Peel cucumber in a striped pattern, then cut into 1 1/2" (3 to 4 cm) pieces. Add salt, stir well, then rinse.
2. In a pot, combine mixture A and heat. Pour onto cucumbers and stir.

The tangy tomatoes and olives are a great match with toast

Ingredients

1 tomato

2 to 3 leaves basil (fresh or dried)

10 black olives

A (x 2)
- 1/2 clove garlic, grated
- 1 Tbsp olive oil
- Pinch salt
- Pepper, to taste
- Baguette (six 1/2" slices)

Instructions

1. Dice the tomato into 1" (2 cm) squares. Cut basil into 1" (2 cm) pieces, and finely chop olives.
2. Combine 2 servings of mixture A in separate bowls. In one bowl, add tomato and basil, and add olives to the other.
3. Serve each topping on toasted baguette slices.

Note

Adding grated garlic and olive oil to toast is also a tasty-yet-simple dish.

Spicy Marinated Turnip

I like this with chili oil

I like to cut the turnips into half-moons and chop up the stems and pile it high in the dish. Add a fair amount of chili oil—use as much as you please. (I use about 15 drops.) The bonito flakes and sesame oil balance out the chili oil's spiciness surprisingly well.

The sesame mellows the tongue-numbing chili oil

Ingredients

5 turnips

1 tsp salt

A
- 2 packs bonito flakes
- 1 tsp soy sauce
- 1 tsp sesame oil
- 1/2 tsp salt
- Chili oil, to taste

Instructions

1. Leaving the skin on, remove the stem from the turnips, then slice into 1/5" (5 mm) half-moons. Chop turnip stems into 2" (5 cm) pieces. Add to a bowl, sprinkle with salt and mix.
2. In a separate bowl, combine mixture A. Rinse turnips, then dry. Add turnips to mixture A and mix.

Marinated Octopus

An easy, chic dish

Seafood can be daunting to an inexperienced cook, but here you can use pre-boiled octopus to make it really easy and quick. This is the perfect seafood dish—simple and healthy, and it packs a great toothsome texture. The olive oil adds balance to the flavors.

Be sure to use wholegrain mustard

Ingredients

1/2 lb (200 g) boiled octopus

1/2 onion

A
- 1 tsp wholegrain mustard
- 1 1/2 Tbsp rice vinegar
- 1 Tbsp olive oil
- 1/2 tsp sugar
- Pinch salt
- Pepper, to taste

Instructions

1. Chop octopus into bite-size pieces. Thinly slice onion along the grain.
2. In a bowl, combine mixture A. Add octopus and onion, and stir.

Squid and *Kimchi*

Enjoy the unique blend of sake and sesame oil

Just mix raw squid sashimi and *kimchi*. I also added the lonely-seeming shredded daikon that always comes with sashimi. The level of spiciness and flavor varies per batch with *kimchi*, so check the flavor repeatedly as you season this dish.

The sesame oil adds fragrance

Ingredients

3 servings sushi-grade squid (thinly sliced, as used for sashimi)

Shredded daikon (used for sashimi)

4/5 C cabbage *kimchi*

A
- 1/2 tsp soy sauce
- 1 tsp sake
- Sesame oil, to taste
- 1 to 2 tsp roasted white sesame seeds

Instructions

1. Cut *kimchi* into 1" (2 cm) squares.
2. In a bowl, combine *kimchi*, squid, daikon and mixture A. Stir well.

Fried Cheese Sticks

Crispy outside, gooey inside

Recipe on page 16

These days you can find at least one shop with a great cheese selection just about anywhere. Some people might not like processed cheese, but it's best for this recipe. That light and salty flavor also has a sweetness, and the way it stays just a little chewy in the middle is fantastic. A simple wrap of dumpling skins does the trick.

Crispy

Now *these* are appetizers! Crispy and crunchy, they go with almost any drink—beer, wine or sake. You can fry them using just a little oil. You'd think a great crispy outside can only come from deep-frying over high heat, but a nice, slow fry over low heat cooks off all the moisture. The perfect partner to a relaxing evening.

Crunchy

Cheese Crackers

Ready once they turn golden

Recipe on page 16

No one will guess that these crackers are just dumpling skins. Ha ha ha! Simply add some cheese and broil. I found that skipping the butter actually made these taste better. Even after cooling, these crackers stay crisp.

Cheese Toast

A perfect crispy treat

Recipe on page 16

To make the most fragrant and tempting cheese toast, use very thin bread and don't butter it before toasting. You can cut the bread into stylish shapes for a pretty presentation.

Fried Cheese Sticks

Be sure to seal up the wrappers tightly

Photo page 14

Ingredients
4 slices 2/5" (1 cm) thick processed cheese
12 dumpling (gyoza) wrappers
Oil, for frying

Instructions
1. Cut each slice of cheese into thirds.
2. Lay a piece of cheese on top of a dumpling wrapper and fold in half. Wet the edges of the wrapper, fold around cheese and pinch ends together. Roll up tightly.
3. In a pan, add 2/5" (1 cm) oil and heat over medium to 320 to 340°F (160 to 170°C). Add cheese sticks and fry until golden brown.

Note
If you don't properly close up the ends of the wrappers, the cheese will melt and leak into the oil. Also, frying in very hot oil will cause them to burst, so add sticks to relatively cool oil. Add flour to the dumpling skin when adding the cheese to help it stick in place.

Cheese Crackers

Once they start to brown, they're done, so keep an eye out!

Photo page 15

Ingredients
Dumpling (gyoza) wrappers, as needed
Powdered Parmesan cheese, as needed

Instructions
Sprinkle dumpling wrappers with Parmesan cheese and and arrange on baking sheet. Broil for 4 to 5 minutes or until golden. Be sure to watch them closely as they brown very quickly.

Cheese Toast

Sprinkle with paprika and curry powder

Photo page 15

Ingredients
2 slices thin sandwich bread
2 slices cheese
Paprika, to taste

Instructions
Place cheese slices on top of bread and place in oven (or toaster oven) to broil. Remove from oven when cheese is melted and slightly browned. Sprinkle with paprika and cut into easy-to-handle pieces. You can use any sliced cheese you like. Just be sure it's a type that's not too sticky when melted.

Fried Mochi

Pair with grated daikon

Photo page 18

Ingredients

4 pieces mochi
1 1/2" (3 to 4 cm) daikon
Soy sauce, as needed
Oil, for frying

Instructions

1. Quarter each mochi and grate daikon.
2. In a pan, add 2/5" (1 cm) oil and heat. Add mochi pieces before oil gets too hot. Fry slowly over low to medium heat until golden brown.
3. Remove from oil, plate, and garnish with grated daikon. Add soy sauce to taste.

Note

Add mochi while the oil is still cool enough to touch.

Crispy Bacon

The quality of the bacon is important

Photo page 18

Ingredients

Bacon, as much as you want
Salt and pepper, to taste

Instructions

1. Add bacon to pan and cook over low heat.
2. While cooking, use a paper towel to drain excess fat. Continue to cook until bacon is crisp.
3. Remove from heat and place on paper towels. Sprinkle with salt and pepper.

Note

Bunch paper towel and blot bacon to soak up excess fat. If you do this, the bacon will crisp up nicely. But if it doesn't crisp, it's not you, it's the bacon. Poor quality bacon doesn't crisp properly. The amount of fat, quality of the meat as well as additives affect the level of crispiness.

Fried Noodles

Add a good amount of salt

Photo page 19

Ingredients

Somen (or vermicelli) noodles, boiled and drained, as needed
Dash salt
A ⌈Pepper, garlic powder, onion powder and
⌊celery powder, to taste
Oil, for frying

Instructions

1. In a frying pan, add 2/5" (1 cm) oil and heat to 320 to 340°F (160 to 170°C).
2. Add noodles and shape into a large mass in the oil. Fry over low heat until golden brown (about 20 minutes). Turn over and fry the other side.
3. Once browned, remove from heat and sprinkle with salt and mixture A.

Potato Skins

Peel thick pieces

Photo page 19

Ingredients

Potatoes, as needed
Salt and pepper, to taste
Oil, for frying

Instructions

1. Rinse potatoes thoroughly and peel thick slices of skin.
2. In a frying pan, add 2/5" (1 cm) oil and heat over medium.
3. Add potato skins and fry over low heat for 5 to 6 minutes or until crispy. When crisped, remove from heat and sprinkle with salt and freshly ground pepper.

Fried Mochi

Quarter and fry slowly on low

Recipe on page 17

Grab a bag of plain mochi and fry away. Quartered mochi blocks are the perfect size, since you want to keep that great gooey center. If the pieces are too small they'll end up very tough.

Crispy Bacon

You'll be surprised by the light, crisp texture

Recipe on page 17

Bacon that's had the excess fat drained is completely different from normally cooked bacon. This bacon is crispy from start to finish. This is the perfect treat to go with a cold beer—a crispy, salty and slightly fatty appetizer.

Fried Noodles

A light crunch

Recipe on page 17

Whenever I have leftover noodles from dinner, I save them for this wonderfully crispy appetizer. Fry slowly over low heat until golden. 3 batches will take about 30 minutes to brown, but if you keep an eye on them while enjoying a drink or making other appetizers, the time flies by and they'll be ready before you know it

Potato Skins

The skins are the best part

Recipe on page 17

Just fry up the skins of potatoes. Buy organic potatoes and put your mind at ease about pesticides. Rinse the skins well before frying and dry well. It's boring if the skins are short, so try peeling off long rounds, like peeling an apple.

19

Hints for Making Great Appetizers

The toaster oven is a good ally

There are a few hints to making delicious appetizers that work with delectable alcoholic beverages.

When you invite people over and begin to serve the hors d'oeuvres, you should consider the order of the entire lineup. What needs to be made first? What will be served first? I always serve the appetizers prepared in advace first, then start cooking. I never get home early enough to prepare it all before my guests arrive, so this method works well for me. My toaster oven is my biggest ally. It can grill sausage, toast thin sheets of tofu, and brown cheese crackers. While the toaster oven does all that work for me, I can cook something else on the stove. It's easy multitasking.

When I'm drinking alone, cooking on the stovetop is tedious, so the toaster oven is a convenient alternative. It's easy to make a small appetizer and pop it in the toaster oven, then kick back and relax because there's nothing left to do!

Pile it high: Presentation

I want to give you a word of advice on plating. Meat dishes look succulent served on a large platter piled high with proteins, while individual dishes make simple marinades and pickles look special. After plating, add a sprinkle of seven-spice powder or black pepper, or try a dash of oil to top it off.

The order in which the appetizers are served is also important. The first appetizer should be light and refreshing, then I suggest slowly progressing towards richer fare. You want the first appetizer to have a good crunch, like fresh vegetables, then move onto something warm. Offer a plate with something tangy or sour, then move on to something heavy. After a small break, end with a rice dish. It's always a good idea to leave a side dish of refreshing pickles out for the duration of the party.

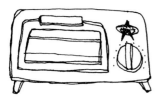

The key is 2/5" (1 cm) oil

There's a trick to frying to make it a lot less tedious. At home, I always fry foods in a frying pan. I fill the pan with just 2/5 to 1/2" of oil. That's all you need. Then, excluding larger foods—eggplant, for example—I fill the pan with the items to be fried. Don't think you have to submerge the ingredients in tons of oil and fry very slowly. The point is to have the tips of whatever you're frying sticking out of the oil. A bit of air contact allows the moisture to cook off, and the result is a light and crispy fried delight. You can fry a lot all at once using only 2/5" of oil, and the cleanup is easy, too. When drinking, oily foods are super satisfying. Washing down something greasy with a nice, cold beer is just amazing. So remember the 2/5" rule with oil. You'll be creating fabulous fried dishes in no time.

Choose drinks to fit the mood

There's a wide variety of drinks to choose from. So how do you narrow down your selection? It's important to have drinks and appetizers that fit the mood. Beer is the all-around player—nothing beats a cold beer with fried foods or a spicy appetizer. Foods that pack a punch go well with an ice-cold beer. There's a plethora of wines to choose from and many inexpensive wines can be very good. Recently, I had a ten dollar bottle of wine from Chile and it was phenomenal. Don't worry too much about pairing white with one dish and red with another. It usually doesn't make that much of a difference, so try them out and see what you like the most. Wine goes great with Japanese cuisine, and hard liquors are a nice match with sweet dishes. With so many beverages—Japanese sake and *shochu* as well—it's so hard to pick just one.

Gotta Have Meat!

It's got to be meat. That aromatic grilled surface, that red juice seeping out, that juicy chunkiness, that savory fattiness—basically everything you need to make the liquor disappear quicker. Everyone loves the tempting sight of a large platter of meat. Just dust with salt, and grill it up. Amazing how something so simple can make people smile.

Wasabi Butter Beef

Medium-cooked beef is good— beef with spicy sauce is even better

Recipe on page 24

This is kind of like a Japanese-style roast beef done in a frying pan. The sauce is a mix of soy sauce, wasabi and butter. A seamless fusion of Western and Japanese styles. Or maybe it's Japanese in spirit but tempered by Western savvy? Choose lean meat, and let it rest before slicing. Cook the meat to medium. This is important.

Wasabi Butter Beef

Heat the pan beforehand for a great-looking steak

Photo page 22

Ingredients

1 lb. (500 g) beef (thigh or other lean cut)
1/2 Tbsp vegetable oil
Dash salt
Pepper, to taste
1 1/2 Tbsp (20 g) butter
2 Tbsp soy sauce
1 tsp wasabi

Instructions

1. In a small pan, melt butter, then add soy sauce and wasabi. Stir well.
2. In a well-heated frying pan, add beef and season with salt and pepper. Cook covered over medium heat until surface is browned. Cook all sides until browned, then remove from pan and let rest. Slice and arrange on serving dish. Serve with sauce from step 1.

Note

If the pan dries out before the beef is browned add more oil. Check the meat with a skewer or toothpick to see if it's done.

Dishing Out the Meat

Meaty appetizers are a crowd pleaser. Fried tofu in broth and vinegared seafood salad are delicious, but when there's a juicy steak on the table, everyone stops to stare, sometimes even forgetting about their drinks.

I think meat is best served piled up high on a large platter. It's not a bad idea to use a fair amount of salt and pepper. As a general rule, appetizers should be well-seasoned, and that's especially true with meat. You don't want the flavor to seem half-hearted. Also, remember that chicken takes a long time to cook. Unlike red meat, the center of chicken needs to be well-done. It's such a bummer to take chicken off the stove and plate it, only to find you need to cook it again. So keep chicken covered and cook completely before serving. Don't worry about a little charring; crispy is fine for appetizers.

A decent slice of fatty pork belly, a hunk of shoulder roast or even beef thigh are all great choices for hors d'oeuvres. Fatty meats that you can't typically serve for the main course are welcome in small portions. Fry over high heat until nice and crispy on the outisde, garnish with a drizzle of sesame oil and serve. I guarantee it'll go well with beer and Japanese *shochu*. Be sure to cook until the center is warm because a cold center is a real turn-off. I promise, a heaping portion of meat is a real winner. When making stir-fry, cook over high heat quickly and flip ingredients in the pan or wok. If you take too long to fry, veggies turn mushy and meat toughens up too much. If you're not comfortable tossing the stir-fry up in the air to mix, use two spatulas, and flip up carefully from the bottom. That's the Kobayashi stir-frying secret.

Ribs with Green Onions

Ribs smothered with soy sauce and green onions

Recipe on page 28

Let the meat sit in the pan and cook thoroughly until browned. Don't worry if some of it gets a little charred. The meat soaks up the rich flavors of the green onions blended with soy sauce. It's okay if the seasoning is on the rich side.

Cube Steak with Garlic

Lots of volume and a very satisfying garlic aroma

Recipe on page 28

This is the answer to your cravings for meat after downing a cold one. It's easy to make, and gives you the singular satisfaction only meat can bring. Cubed meat doesn't need to be browned on every side, so don't let it roll around too much when cooking.

Salted Cow Tongue

A healthy dose of salt is all you need!

Recipe on page 29

Most people only eat cow tongue at *yakiniku* restaurants, but try making this at home. Place tongue in a well-heated pan and cook thoroughly. It'll come out just as good as when it's cooked over an open flame. Just make sure it's well-seasoned with salt! Anyone and everyone is thrilled with an appetizer like this.

Beef and Chive Stir-fry

The powerful garlic fragrance is super tantalizing

Recipe on page 29

It's as easy as one, two, three—just give it a quick toss in a wok and it's out on the table. The rich flavor comes from lots of garlic and chives. Use well-marbled end cuts, since those are perfect for soaking in the flavor. The fattier the better (and cheaper)!

Ribs with Green Onions

Heat pan until smoke rises and the oil practically jumps out

Photo page 26

Ingredients
14 oz (400 g) beef ribs
1 green onion (or leek)

A
- 2 Tbsp soy sauce
- 1 Tbsp roasted white sesame seeds
- 1 Tbsp sesame oil
- 1/2 Tbsp mirin (sweet cooking wine)
- 1 clove garlic, grated

1/2 Tbsp sesame oil

Instructions
1. Finely chop green onion. Combine mixture A in a bowl and add green onion, then mix. Add ribs and allow to marinate for 5 minutes.
2. Add sesame oil to a well-heated pan. Start with high heat. Flip and cook other side. Let fry mostly undisturbed until both sides are well-browned.

Note
Feel free to add Doubanjiang or chili sauce to the marinade if you like.

Cube Steak with Garlic

Fry until browned in garlic-infused oil

Photo page 26

Ingredients
7 to 8 oz (200 to 250 g) beef steak
2 to 3 cloves garlic
Dash salt
Pepper, to taste
1 Tbsp vegetable oil
1/2 Tbsp soy sauce

Instructions
1. Dice steak into 1 1/4" (3 cm) cubes. Thinly slice garlic into 1/8" (2 to 3 mm) pieces.
2. In a pan, add oil and sauté garlic over low heat until golden and crispy.
3. Remove garlic from pan and set aside. Reheat pan and add steak and season with salt and pepper. Cook top side and bottom of steak pieces over high, but don't roll steak around too much.
4. Once browned, add soy sauce and stir. Serve on a dish garnished with fried garlic and pepper.

Note
Cubed steak will have six sides but you only need to cook two sides for medium-level doneness. You can always brown two sides well then give the other sides a quick fry, but don't roll the steak around too much.

Salted Cow Tongue

Brown thoroughly on a well-heated pan

Photo page 27

Ingredients

7 oz (200 g) cow tongue, thinly sliced
1/2 green onion (or leek)
1 Tbsp roasted white sesame seeds
1 tsp salt
Pepper, to taste
1 tsp vegetable oil
Lemon, to taste

Instructions

1. Lay out slices of tongue and sprinkle with salt and pepper. Chop green onion into rounds.
2. In a well-heated pan, add vegetable oil, then tongue slices. Fry over high heat until browned on both sides.
3. Serve on a dish and garnish with green onion and sesame seeds. Add a squeeze of lemon on top.

Beef and Chive Stir-fry

Lots and lots of aromatic ingredients

Photo page 27

Ingredients

7 oz (200 g) end-cut (fatty) beef
1 bunch garlic chives
1 clove garlic
1 nub ginger
1 Tbsp sake
1/2 Tbsp soy sauce
1/2 Tbsp oyster sauce
Dash salt
Pepper, to taste
1 Tbsp sesame oil

Instructions

1. Cut chives into 1 1/2" (3 to 4 cm) pieces. Mince garlic and ginger.
2. Add sesame oil to a well-heated wok, then add garlic and ginger. Add beef to pan quickly after, before garlic and ginger burn, and turn heat up to high. Sprinkle with pepper.
3. When the beef starts to brown, add chives and salt. When chives are tender, add sake, soy sauce and oyster sauce, and stir to coat. Season with salt gradually while checking flavor.

Sunny-Side Up Beef

A dense, rich flavor that's pleasantly smooth

Recipe on page 32

A definite must-try delight. Creamy egg yolk coats the sweet-and-spicy thin slices of beef. Coat each forkful of meat with the yolk and enjoy. I love this dish. Just thinking about it makes me want to eat it tonight. It's perfection when paired with a cup of sake.

Salted Chicken

Shake that salt shaker!

Recipe on page 33

This is pan-fried yakitori. Be generous with the salt and mix well. Heat up the pan. Line up the chicken pieces skin-down and fry over high heat while draining off any excess fat. A delectable dish, the crispy, salty skin is what makes this a hit every time.

Chicken Meatball and Miso Stew

A rustic, relaxing flavor

Recipe on page 33

You don't have to worry about making any broth beforehand. Just take the chicken and make it into meatballs, then drop them in the water to cook. Don't worry about keeping an eye on it—just have a glass of sake or make other appetizers. The chicken won't dry out even if you let it simmer for a long time. That's what makes chicken a great choice for meatballs.

Sunny-Side Up Beef

Well-seasoned and served with a fresh egg

Photo page 30

Ingredients

7 oz (200 g) beef roast, sliced 1/5" (5 mm) thick
2 tsp sesame oil

A ⎡ 1 Tbsp soy sauce
⎢ 1 Tbsp sake
⎢ 1 Tbsp mirin (sweet cooking wine)
⎣ 1/2 to 1 Tbsp sugar

1 egg yolk

Instructions

1. Slice beef thinly along the grain. In a bowl, combine mixture A.
2. Add sesame oil to a well-heated pan. Add meat and stir-fry over high heat until browned. Once cooked, add mixture A and stir to coat.
3. Serve on plate and place egg yolk on top. Mix yolk and beef while eating.

Note

You don't need an expensive cut of beef, but be sure to choose a fairly thick cut that has a decent amount of marbling. When slicing, be sure to cut along the grain. If you cut against the grain the beef will crumble when you stir-fry it.

Salted Chicken

Even cheap cuts of chicken come out light, tender and delicious

Photo page 31

Ingredients

7 to 10 oz (200 to 300 g) chicken thigh, skin on
1 tsp salt
Pepper, to taste
2 tsp vegetable oil
Seven-spice powder, to taste

Instructions

1. Remove fat from chicken and dice into 1 1/4" (3 cm) cubes. Sprinkle with salt.
2. In a well-heated pan, add oil and chicken with skin facing down and fry over high heat.
3. When the skin has browned turn over in pan and cook the other side covered over medium-low heat.
4. Insert a skewer into a piece of chicken. If no cloudy liquid or blood comes out, turn heat to high. Blot excess liquid from chicken with a paper towel, and sprinkle with seven-spice powder.

Chicken Meatball and Miso Stew

To make light, fluffy meatballs, stir raw meat mixture well

Photo page 31

Ingredients

7 oz (200 g) ground chicken
2 stalks green onion (or leek)
1/2 block tofu
A ⎰ 1 Tbsp potato (or corn) starch
   ⎱ 1 tsp roasted white sesame seeds
   ⎱ 1/2 nub ginger, grated
   ⎱ Japanese (*sansho*) pepper, to taste
3 1/4 C (800 ml) water
3 to 4 Tbsp miso
Seven-spice powder, to taste

Instructions

1. Mince 1/2 of one green onion, then slice the remaining green onions on the bias. Cut tofu into large chunks.
2. In a bowl, add minced green onion, chicken and mixture A. Stir very thoroughly.
3. Bring water to a boil. Take 2 spoons and shape chicken mixture into a ball, then drop into water. Repeat.
4. Simmer over medium heat while removing any foam that floats to the surface. Once meatballs are cooked add sliced green onions and tofu. Simmer briefly, then add miso while repeatedly checking flavor. Finish with seven-spice powder.

Note

Use a dark miso (like haccho) that's rich in flavor.

Cha Shao
Definitely use shoulder roast!

Recipe on page 36

One of the best parts of making *cha shao*-style pork yourself is the fact that you can cut thick, juicy slices. This particular recipe, featuring a honey-based sauce, is my personal pride and joy. But definitely use a shoulder cut. I've tried this before with leg meat and it dried out and fell apart.

Pork and Green Onion Sesame Stir-fry

A winning combination of green onion and mounds of sesame

Recipe on page 36

I originally used this green onion-sesame-soy sauce as dressing for udon noodles. I found that it works very well in stir-fries as well. The blend of sweet pork, crisp green onion and fragrant cracked sesame makes my mouth water for a glass of Japanese *shochu*.

Pork Strips with Salty Sauc

Pork belly crisped in its own rendered fat

Recipe on page 37

Now you might be thinking, what's with the sauce? It's just a simple combo of salt and sesame oil to create a scrumptious dipping sauce. This lets you enjoy the rich sesame flavor full-on. The rich flavor soaks into the fatty pork. Tasting is believing with this perfect appetizer-only pairing.

Shabu Pork with Onion

Pork belly can be surprisingly light

Recipe on page 37

I think many people use pork roast for *shabu-shabu*, but I use pork belly. I think it's unexpectedly refreshing, mellow and tastier than your average roast.

95

Cha Shao

Add water while boiling and make sure it's cooked completely

Photo page 34

Ingredients
14 oz (400 g) pork shoulder roast
1 green onion (green part)
1 clove garlic
1 nub ginger

A ┌ 1/4 C soy sauce
  │ 1 clove garlic, grated
  │ 1 Tbsp honey
  └ Dash sesame oil

Instructions
1. In a bowl, combine mixture A and set aside.
2. Halve ginger and garlic.
3. In a pot, bring ample water to a boil and add pork, green onion, garlic and ginger. Cook over medium heat for 40 to 50 minutes or until no cloudy liquid comes out when a skewer is inserted into the pork.
4. Once pork is cooked, drain, then add to bowl with mixture A. Let marinate for 20 minutes.
5. Slice pork to desired thickness and serve.

Pork and Green Onion Sesame Stir-fry

The only fussy part is chopping the sesame seeds beforehand

Photo page 35

Ingredients
7 oz (200 g) pork roast
2 green onions (or leeks)
2 Tbsp cracked white sesame seeds
1 Tbsp soy sauce
1 Tbsp sesame oil

Instructions
1. Slice green onions on the bias into thin rounds and cut pork into large bite-size pieces.
2. Add sesame oil to a well-heated pan, then add pork and stir-fry over high heat.
3. When the pork is browned add green onions, sesame seeds, and soy sauce, then sauté briefly.

Note
To bring out the aroma of the sesame seeds, either chop or crush the sesame seeds with a knife.

Pork Strips with Salty Sauce

Use thick slices of pork—otherwise it'll shrivel up in the pan

Photo page 35

Ingredients
10 1/2 oz (300 g) pork belly, sliced to 1/5" (5 mm)
2 to 3 Tbsp sesame oil
1 heaping Tbsp salt
1 tsp vegetable oil

Instructions
1. Cut pork into bite-size pieces.
2. Combine sesame oil and salt.
3. Add vegetable oil to a well-heated pan, then add meat. Fry over high heat on both sides until browned.
4. Serve pork with salty sauce on the side.

Note
If the pork is too thin, it'll shrivel up. 1/5" slices are a good thickness, even a little bigger is fine. A lot of fat ends up rendered in the pan, so siphon it off with a paper towel. This way the pork will have a nice crisp finish. For the sauce, use so much salt that it rises above the surface of the sesame oil like an iceberg.

Shabu Pork with Onion

Boil the pork all at once—it's pork belly, so it'll stay tender no matter what

Photo page 35

Ingredients
10 1/2 oz (300 g) pork belly
1 cucumber
1 green onion (or leek)
2 to 3 Tbsp soy sauce
Dash grated garlic

Instructions
1. Slice pork into bite-size pieces. Pound cucumber using the flat of a knife, then score them and break into pieces. Add a dash of salt and blend into cucumbers.
2. Finely chop green onion, then mix with soy sauce and grated garlic.
3. Bring lightly salted water to a rolling boil. Add pork and boil thoroughly. Once pork is done, drain in a colander.
4. Serve pork on a dish on top of cucumbers and finish with sauce from step 2.

Note
Pork belly stays tender even if it's a little over-cooked, so go ahead and boil it all at once. It couldn't be easier.

Romaine and Sesame Salad

The grated onion gives it an extra kick

Recipe on page 40

Dress it up, Pile it on

These are so easy, they're impossible to mess up. If you have just one bowl and one pot, you can whip up these versatile dishes—keep it simple or add a twist, either is fine. Don't stress over cutting everything exactly the same size. When you feel like you want just one more appetizer simply dress it up, mix it up and pile it on. Since it's simple, don't skimp on the presentation!

Shrimp and Avocado with Wasabi Mayonnaise

Even though there's a lot of wasabi, it doesn't sting your nose

Recipe on page 40

38

Cream Cheese and Dried Fruits Salad

Sweet, but not too sweet

Recipe on page 41

Broccoli and Cauliflower Salad

An acidic dressing with mellow Parmesan is delicious

Recipe on page 41

Romaine and Sesame Salad

Tear off big chunks of lettuce

Photo page 38

This is similar to the salads you can find at *yakiniku* restaurants. The bitterness of the lettuce blends nicely with the sharp grated onion for a unique flavor. You can always add some boiled octopus or shellfish on top for a more filling bite.

Ingredients

1 head romaine lettuce

A
- 1 Tbsp grated onion
- 1/2 clove grated garlic
- 1 Tbsp soy sauce
- 1 Tbsp sesame oil
- 1 Tbsp sesame seed
- Pepper to taste

Instructions

1. Tear lettuce into bite-size pieces.
2. Combine mixture A, then pour over lettuce.

Shrimp and Avocado with Wasabi Mayonnaise

Boil the shrimp shell-on for extra flavor

Photo page 38

I love avocados. There was a time when I would eat one almost every day. One day I wondered if it was possible to create an avocado appetizer. This is what I came up with. Not bad, eh? You can make it as a meal or an appetizer—just be sure not to skimp on the wasabi.

Ingredients

1 avocado
5 to 6 large shrimp or prawns
Dash lemon juice

A
- 1 Tbsp mayonnaise
- 1/2 to 1 Tbsp soy sauce
- 1 tsp wasabi

Instructions

1. Remove skin and pit from avocado and cut into 1" (2 cm) cubes. Sprinkle lemon juice on top to keep avocado from oxidizing. Devein shrimp, boil in lightly salted water then remove shells. Slice in half lengthwise.
2. In a bowl, combine mixture A. Add avocado and shrimp and stir.

Cream Cheese and Dried Fruits Salad

Give it a boost by adding crunchy nuts

Photo page 39

I created this appetizer as an accompaniment to whiskey or brandy. Chocolate is a great match for European liquors, and I found myself craving something small but densely flavored to go with my drink. This appetizer is a hit with my friends who like to savor their alcohol.

Ingredients
3 1/2 oz (100 g) cream cheese
5 to 6 dried apricots
3 dried prunes
1 Tbsp raisins
10 pistachios
Dash rum liquor

Instructions
1. Dice cream cheese into 1" cubes. Quarter apricots and prunes. Shell pistachios and slice in half.
2. Combine ingredients in a bowl and serve.

Broccoli and Cauliflower Salad

Fresh veggies blanched briefly in well-salted water

Photo page 39

The garlic-based dressing blends well with the rich Parmesan cheese. If you chill it in the fridge, the vinegar seeps in and mellows out the cheese for a wonderfully rich flavor in every bite. Use the stem of the broccoli as well for a hearty, healthy crunch.

Ingredients
1 head broccoli
1 head cauliflower
A ⎰ 1 clove garlic, grated
⎰ 1 to 2 Tbsp olive oil
⎰ 2 Tbsp rice vinegar
⎰ 2 pinches salt
⎰ Pepper, to taste
1 Tbsp grated Parmesan cheese

Instructions
1. Cut the cauliflower and broccoli florets into bite-size pieces. Peel broccoli stem and cut into 2" (4 to 5 cm) pieces. Blanch cauliflower and broccoli florets in salted boiling water.
2. In a bowl, combine mixture A. Drain cauliflower and broccoli then add to dressing. Add Parmesan cheese and stir lightly.

Daikon with Plum

Leave the skin on for a toothsome crunch

Recipe on page 44

This dish is all about a big, satisfying crunch. The daikon should be sprinkled with salt. It's an easily-forgotten-but-still-important step. If you forget the salt, the daikon will be soggy. And who wants soggy daikon?

Daikon with Hot Sesame Oil

The delicate flavors are sure to please any palate

Recipe on page 44

Thinly slice daikon and soak it in soy sauce, then douse with a bit of well-heated sesame oil. Adding salt to the daikon beforehand will allow the flavors to soak in more thoroughly.

Crunchy
Daikon Salad
Slice along the grain!

Recipe on page 44

Daikon sliced along the grain has an excellent crunch. Light, refreshing dressings go best with this root vegetable. And don't forget the *shiso*! For some reason, when you slice up daikon this way, it seems like you end up with more than you started with. True story!

Tender
Daikon Salad
Slice against the grain!

Recipe on page 44

This version uses daikon sliced against the grain, giving it a very different texture. I've combined the tender daikon with canned scallops. Scallops can be very heavy, but the addition of grated ginger helps keep those chopsticks going.

Daikon with Plum

Sesame oil is necessary to balance out the sourness of the pickled plum

Photo page 42

Ingredients

2" (5 cm) daikon
1/2 tsp salt
1 large pickled plum (*umeboshi*)
1/2 tsp soy sauce
1/2 tsp sesame oil

Instructions

1. Peel daikon and cut into 1/5" (5 mm) thick slices. Add daikon to a bowl and sprinkle with salt and stir.
2. Remove pit from plum and finely chop.
3. Rinse daikon and pat dry. In a bowl, add daikon, plum, soy sauce and sesame oil, and stir.

Daikon with Hot Sesame Oil

Use lots of sesame oil

Photo page 42

Ingredients

2 to 2 1/2" (5 to 6 cm) daikon
1/2 tsp salt
A ⌈ 1 Tbsp soy sauce
⌊ 1/2 tsp sake
⌊ Roasted white sesame seeds, to taste
2 Tbsp sesame oil

Instructions

1. Peel daikon and cut into slices. Place daikon in a bowl and sprinkle with salt and stir.
2. Rinse daikon and dry. In a bowl, combine mixture A, add daikon and mix.
3. Pour sesame oil into a small pot and heat on stove.
4. Serve daikon on a dish and pour heated sesame oil on top.

Crunchy Daikon Salad

Add dressing just before serving

Photo page 43

Ingredients

2 1/2" (5 to 6 cm) daikon
A few *shiso* leaves (daikon leaves are OK, too)
A ⌈ 1/2 Tbsp soy sauce, 1 Tbsp rice vinegar
⌊ 1/2 Tbsp olive oil, Pinch salt
Dash pepper

Instructions

1. Peel daikon and slice along the grain into 1/5" (5 mm) thick pieces, then julienne lengthwise. Soak in water. Finely chop shiso.
2. In a bowl, combine mixture A. Pat daikon dry and add to bowl, then stir. Serve on a dish, garnish with *shiso* and season with pepper.

Tender Daikon Salad

The ginger is more potent than you think

Photo page 43

Ingredients

2 to 2 1/2" (5 to 6 cm) daikon
Dash chopped scallions
1 can (2 1/2 oz (70 g)) scallops
A ⌈ Dash grated ginger
⌊ 1/2 Tbsp lemon juice
⌊ 1 Tbsp mayonnaise
⌊ Pinch salt
Small amount of canning liquid from scallops

Instructions

1. Peel daikon and cut widthwise into rounds 1/5" (5 mm) thick, then julienne. Chop scallions into small rounds.
2. In a bowl, combine mixure A. Add scallops and a small amount of canning liquid, then add daikon and scallions. Stir until evenly mixed.

Fried Tofu with Miso

Add extra flavor with seven-spice powder or fresh garlic

Photo page 46

Ingredients

1 sheet *aburaage* (thin fried tofu)
2 Tbsp chopped scallions

A ⎰ 1 tsp miso
   1 tsp mirin (sweet cooking wine)
   1 tsp sake
   Dash sesame oil

Instructions

1. In a bowl, combine scallions and mixture A.
2. Brush mixture onto tofu then cook in toaster oven (or broiler) until browned.

Potato with *Kimchi*

Taste the kimchi before mixing

Photo page 47

Ingredients

3 potatoes (14 to 17 oz (400 to 500 g))
3 1/2 oz Napa cabbage *kimchi*
1/4 sac *tarako* (pollock roe)
Dash sesame oil

Instructions

1. Peel potatoes and cut into bite-size pieces. Add potatoes and ample water to a pot. Simmer, covered, for about ten minutes or until a skewer can be easily inserted.
2. Chop *kimchi*. Remove membrane from *tarako* and crumble.
3. Mix ingredients from steps 1 and 2 together, add sesame oil and stir.

Potato with *Tarako* Butter

A simple, buttery flavor

Photo page 47

Ingredients

3 potatoes (14 to 17 oz (400 to 500 g))
1 sac *tarako* (pollock roe)
2 Tbsp butter

Instructions

1. Peel potatoes and cut into 2/5" (1 cm) rounds. Add potatoes and water to a pot. Simmer for about 10 minutes or until a skewer can be easily inserted.
2. Set butter aside until it reaches room temperature. Remove membrane from *tarako* and add to butter. Mix thoroughly.
3. Lay potato slices on a serving dish and spread *tarako* butter on top.

Note

1 sac of *tarako* contains 2 pieces.

Fried Tofu with Miso

Pop it in the toaster oven for a few minutes

Recipe on page 45

Smother *aburaage* with miso and scallions, then toast. This is a delicious treat that will awaken your taste buds. Miso alone can be too salty and tough to work with, so mix a dash of mirin and a dollop of rice wine to smooth out the flavor. Remember this trick for miso-based stir-fries as well.

Potato with *Kimchi*

Spicy and scrumptious

Recipe on page 45

Just a simple dish of boiled potatoes blended with pollock roe and spicy cabbage *kimchi*. All the flavors balance out nicely. A dash of sesame oil adds a gentleness that broadens the flavor spectrum.

Potato with *Tarako* Butter

This'll change your perception of potatoes forever

Recipe on page 45

Potatoes mixed with *tarako* is a popular item at bars and pubs in Japan. But this version turns the well-loved staple into a canapé-style finger food. The simple spread of *tarako* mixed with butter is simply delicious.

Crowd Pleasers

You can't go wrong with these go-to appetizers. It's always comforting to have some well-tested regulars on the table. Our family-secret chicken-frying technique is a definite winner. I even have a special trick I use for boiled edamame. You can throw these dishes together in a hurry or prepare them ahead of time and let the flavors stew. And your friends are sure to love 'em. They'll say, "Can't skip these," as they go to refill their glass.

1   2   3   4   5

Use a small amount of oil and fry skin-side down

Photo page 49

Ingredients

3 boneless chicken thighs, skin on

A
- 2 Tbsp soy sauce
- 1 tsp sake
- 1 tsp sesame oil
- 1 clove garlic, grated
- Dash ginger juice

1/2 C potato (or corn) starch

Oil, for frying

Instructions

1. Remove excess fat and gristle from ends of chicken thighs. Use kitchen scissors if necessary.
2. Cut chicken into 2" (5 cm) pieces. This size lets the chicken plump up nicely. Combine mixture A, add chicken and massage seasonings in thoroughly.
3. Add chicken to a bowl and coat thoroughly with potato starch. Starch works better than flour, as flour tends to clump and taste grainy. Press starch into chicken.
4. Add 2/5" (1 cm) oil to a pan and heat over medium. Stretch out skin and place chicken skin-side down. If the tops of the chicken pieces are above the surface of the oil, the moisture evaporates faster and it fries up better. When chicken is almost done, turn heat up to high for a crisp finish. Poke chicken with a skewer. If juices run clear, it's done.
5. Remove chicken from pan and set on a wire rack to drain and cool. Add chicken pieces to rack starting at the back and go forward. This is important, as it keeps excess oil from dripping all over chicken already on the rack. Place chicken skin-side up and keep pieces from overlapping. This allows all excess oil to drain away.

Fried Chicken

Tender meat inside, crispy crunchy outside

Recipe on page 48

Everyone has their own fried chicken recipe—and no two are ever the same. Not to toot my own horn, but my recipe is exceptional. There's a special trick I use that goes against the established rules on frying food. Fill the pan edge-to-edge with chicken, then add just enough oil, leaving the tops of the chicken above the surface. That's the Kobayashi fried chicken secret.

Tomato Salad

Big chunks of juicy tomatoes

Delicious tomatoes deserve delicious dressings. Makes sense, doesn't it? Here you have a choice of dressings: a Western-style simple and refreshing blend of onion and garlic, or Japanese-style, with a little kick of grated ginger and sesame oil. Having more than one option is always appetizing.

Use super-ripe, fresh tomatoes

Ingredients

Japanese-style

2 tomatoes

2 *shiso* leaves, finely chopped

A ⌈ 1/2 nub ginger, grated
⌊ 1 Tbsp sesame oil, 1 Tbsp soy sauce
1/2 Tbsp rice vinegar, dash pepper

Western-style

2 tomatoes

1/2 onion, finely chopped

A ⌈ Dash grated garlic, 1 Tbsp olive oil,
⌊ 1 Tbsp rice vinegar, pinch salt, dash pepper

Instructions

1. Remove stems from tomatoes.
2. Make sure to use a sharp knife and insert tip before slicing through. For Western-style, slice the tomatoes into rounds 1/3" (7 to 8 mm) thick.
3. For Japanese-style, dice tomatoes into 1" (2 to 3 cm) cube or larger, depending on your preference.
4. Combine A mixtures separately. The Japanese dressing (right in photo) will have a fragrant base of ginger and shiso. After adding onions, set aside Western-style dressing (left) allow flavors to blend.

Serving: Japanese-style: Combine tomatoes and dressing. Western-style: Arrange tomatoes on dish and add onions and dressing on top.

1   2   3   4

German Potatoes

Well-cooked, fragrant onions are a necessary part of this dish

1   2   3   4

This is a treasured appetizer that can be found at beer gardens. Give your guests a world-class dish made right in your own kitchen. Since there's only a dash of salt and pepper, the bacon and onions are the main flavor components. Fry up the bacon, then add the potato slices. I recommend using starchy potatoes and cooking until they're light and fluffy.

Add tasty butter partway through

Ingredients

3 potatoes
1/2 onion
3 to 4 slices bacon
1 to 2 tsp butter
2 pinches salt
Pepper, to taste

Instructions

Preparation: Peel potatoes and slice into rounds 2/5" (1 cm) thick. Soak in water for a few minutes. Cut bacon into 1" (2 cm) pieces and finely slice onion.

1. Add potatoes and water to a pot and heat over high. Cover with a lid once water reaches a boil. You'll be sautéing them later so don't boil potatoes until they fall apart. Remove from heat when a skewer can be inserted fairly easily.

2. In a frying pan, add bacon and fry over low heat. When enough fat from the bacon has liquified, add onions. The onions will soak up the bacon-y goodness.

3. Stir-fry onions until they're almost burned. If you fry them over high heat they'll burn quickly, so cook slowly over low heat until browned. Add butter, then add potatoes.

4. After adding potatoes, don't stir them too much while they cook. When potatoes are lightly browned and fragrant, season with salt and pepper.

When the pork is browned, add *kimchi*

Ingredients
7 oz (200 g) pork roast, thinly sliced
7 oz (200 g) Napa cabbage *kimchi*
1 green onion, minced
1 clove garlic, minced
1 nub ginger, minced
1 Tbsp sesame oil
1/2 Tbsp soy sauce
Dash salt
Pepper, to taste
1 Tbsp roasted white sesame seeds

Instructions
Preparation: Cut pork into large bite-size pieces and roughly chop *kimchi*.

1. To prepare green onion, first make several slices along the grain, then mince width-wise.
2. Infusing the sesame oil with garlic and ginger is important. To do this, add the ginger and garlic to the oil in the pan while still cool, then heat over low. This technique can be used in other recipes. Once the oil is fragrant, add the onions.
3. When onions are tender, add pork and turn heat to high. Cook until browned. Add *kimchi* only after pork is thoroughly cooked. If you add it too early, the meat will turn rubbery and the juices from the *kimchi* will water everything down.
4. Season with salt and pepper, add roasted sesame seeds and stir-fry over high heat. Lastly, don't forget to add the soy sauce to enhance the fragrance of the dish.

Pork and *Kimchi*

Taken to the next level with onion, garlic and ginger

To make this quick, fool-proof appetizer, all you need to do is stir-fry some pork and *kimchi*. And voilà! There you have it. However, the spiciness and flavor of *kimchi* tends to vary from one batch to another, so hedge your bets with a little extra seasonings. Everyone needs a little help sometime. I suggest recruiting onion, garlic and ginger.

Salted Fava Beans and Edamame

Here's the secret to making perfectly plump beans

You might think it's condescending of me to teach you how to do something as simple as boil edamame, but I've got a couple of useful tricks I'd like to share: I use just 1 cup of water. Also, I add cold water to the beans, and turn on the heat after that. One of my friends said my edamame are the best, and he was totally shocked to hear that I use just 1 cup of water. It's true, I swear! If you think I'm lying, try it out and see for yourself.

Remove from heat, give it a stir, then let it steam

Ingredients

Fava Beans
3 packs fava beans
  (20 to 25 beans)
1 heaping tsp salt
1 C water

Edamame
1 pack edamame
1 tsp salt
1 C water

Instructions

1. Use about 1 C water, and about 1 tsp salt.
2. The amount of water and boiling method are the same for both sets of beans.
3. The water should be barely visible, right under the beans. But don't worry, it's plenty. And I always start with cold water.
4. Bring to a boil over high, cover, and boil for 5 to 6 minutes. Turn off heat, stir quickly, then cover again. Allow to steam briefly, then drain in a colander. Sprinkle edamame with salt and stir.

1 2 3

Grilled Shiitake Mushrooms

Let the oil soak in, then toast 'em in the oven

Grilled shiitake mushrooms, when done right, are quite juicy on the inside. You don't want to cook them so much they shrivel up. The trick is to let the oil soak into the mushrooms before you grill them. I recommend using sesame oil because it's so fragrant. But be sure to cook the shiitakes well enough that the moisture burns off. Don't rinse the mushrooms before grilling—just wipe with a dry towel to remove any dirt.

Try boiling with pepper for an extra punch

Ingredients
6 fresh shiitake mushrooms
1 Tbsp sesame oil
Soy sauce, to taste
Seven-spice powder, to taste

Instructions
1. Add shiitakes to a bowl and pour sesame oil on top. The stems are also yummy, so only cut off the root ends of the stems. Slice mushrooms in half.
2. Lay mushrooms on a sheet of aluminum foil, then place in toaster oven. No need to flip over while grilling.
3. When browned (appx. 5 minutes), remove from oven. Be careful not to overcook them, as they'll turn tough.
Serving: Plate and finish with soy sauce and seven-spice powder.

1   2   3   4

Fried Eggplant
Fry over high heat and remove from oil fast

Oil and eggplant play well together, but if fried too long the eggplant ends up too oily. The best way to avoid this is by cooking the eggplant quickly over high heat and taking it out of the oil just as soon as it's cooked through. If you let it go too long, the eggplant will end up too greasy.

When the sliced sides puff up, they're ready

Ingredients

6 small eggplants (the slender Japanese or Italian variety)

A
- 1 1/2 Tbsp soy sauce
- 1 tsp mirin (sweet cooking wine)
- 1 tsp sake
- 1 tsp sesame oil
- 1 nub ginger, grated

Oil, for frying

Instructions

1. Quarter eggplants, then soak in heavily salted water for 3 to 4 minutes. This draws out the eggplants' bitter liquid while also preventing them from absorbing too much oil in the pan.
2. Drain and pat dry to remove excess water.
3. Make sure there's room enough in the pan for the eggplants. If they're squished together they turn an ugly color. Keep oil at a medium temperature and the flame on medium to high. Once the cut sides of the eggplant puff up, they're done. Remove from oil quickly.
4. In a bowl, combine mixture A and pour over fried eggplants.

56

Fried Riceballs

So easy, yet so satisfying

Even after a long night of drinking and eating, it's hard to turn down the temptation of a soy sauce-glazed fried riceball. They can be very hard to cook perfectly on a grill, since grains of rice fall off easily or gaps and cracks fill up with too much soy sauce. So I always use a frying pan to whip up these easy, tasty treats.

Baste both sides twice with soy sauce

Ingredients (yields 5)

5 small servings cooked rice
1 tsp sesame oil
Soy sauce, as needed

Instructions

1. Wet your hands before making riceballs so they don't stick to your hands. A triangle shape is easy to eat. If you prep these before you start drinking, you can save time later on.

2. Add sesame oil to a heated pan. Add riceballs and fry both sides over medium heat. The riceballs tend to fall apart if you flip them with chopsticks, so I recommend wetting your hands and turning them over by hand.

3. Once rice is lightly crisped, baste the browned sides of riceballs with soy sauce, then flip over and baste opposite sides. Cook over low heat, as if drying the soy sauce, then flip to other side and baste again with soy sauce. Flip once more and baste second side again. Don't coat the entire riceball with soy sauce, as it will be too salty. Two coats on both sides give the perfect amount. When both sides are crispy and browned remove from heat.

Corned Beef and Cabbage

Whole cabbage simmered in natural sweetness

Recipe on page 62

A friend of mine who loves the great outdoors introduced me to this dish. An easy yet surprisingly hearty mini-meal, just put all the ingredients in a pot and simmer with the lid on tightly. Let the flavors stew for a good 15 minutes. If you like your cabbage very tender, boil a little longer.

All You Need

58

Salted Cabbage

The irresistible sliced ginger is what keeps this from getting dull

Recipe on page 62

How can just a simple dash of salt turn cabbage all sweet and juicy? This is a great, refreshing palate-cleanser to serve. You'll be surprised how much your guests can polish off, and they'll get their fill of good vegetable nutrition.

is Cabbage

When your refrigerator is just about empty, use up that last bit of cabbage to create these delectable appetizers. You can always throw together a quick dish using leftover cabbage and whatever you have lying around. Cabbage is so versatile, it can work in either light and refreshing preparations or you can simmer it for a richer flavor. Whatever type of dish you make—Japanese, Chinese, or Western—there's always a drink that will create a great match. With these recipes, you'll be glad that you bought a whole head.

Cabbage and Clams Garlic Sauté

The clams add a subtle flavor

Recipe on page 62

Cabbage, clams and garlic—a harmonious trio of flavors. Clams have a real fighting spirit, and here their power is fully unleashed. Make sure not to overcook the cabbage, as you'll want to keep that crispy, toothsome texture. Chop it up and stir-fry lightly.

59

Chinese-style Ham and Cabbage

A simple dish with a traditional Chinese sauce

Recipe on page 63

Heat up the dressing and pour it over the cabbage leaves. The rich aroma will try to tempt you into gobbling this down in one bite, but it's fairly heavy, so pace yourself. Salt the cabbage to prepare, but make sure to rinse thoroughly before adding. Otherwise, it'll be way too salty.

Buttered Cabbage

Lots of buttery grilled goodness

Recipe on page 63

The cabbage is nice and crisp, yet soft and mellow. A delicious contradiction. And be sure to give thanks to butter, for lending that uniquely tempting fragrance to simple grilled cabbage.

Fried Cabbage Patty

Drizzle with Worcestershire sauce for added flavor

Recipe on page 63

A deceptively simple cabbage-centric dish that can easily feed a big group. The juicy cabbage alone is enough for a satisfying appetizer, but if you have leftover sausage or bacon sitting sadly in the back of your fridge, add in with the cabbage for an even more filling treat.

Tofu and Bell Pepper Salad

The different textures make for a very interesting bite

Recipe on page 66

The fragrance and fresh crunch of green bell peppers suit tofu very well. I think the sesame seeds and baby sardines tie everything together, making this combination of soft tofu and crisp peppers work very well.

Tofu Steak

A light coat of flour is the key

Recipe on page 66

When I was young, I remember being disappointed when one night the main dish for dinner turned out to be tofu steak. But I was secretly surprised by how scrumptious it was once I actually tried it. My mom's tofu steak was seasoned with soy sauce and ginger. Mine is a variation with butter and garlic-infused soy sauce.

Tofu with Chives

Lots of chives and grated daikon!

Recipe on page 66

Chives are an easy way to turn plain tofu into a tempting appetizer. Just add a mound of chopped chives and you're ready to go. Here I add grated daikon and a dollop of soy sauce to pump up the flavor. Keep the pieces of tofu on the large side for a more appealing presentation.

Chinese-style *Hiyayakko*

The fragrance of warm sesame oil is invigorating

Recipe on page 66

I like using the trick of pouring heated sesame oil on top of chilled silken tofu. It's best to douse it with oil right before serving. Sesame oil and silken tofu are a match made in appetizer heaven.

Almighty Tofu

Tofu is light and subtle, and yet it goes well with practically any type of drink. It smells great when grilled and is tasty with a drizzle of oil, too. Just be wary of too much excess moisture. Rather than place a cutting board on top of a block of tofu to press it, just quickly blanch in boiling water. At the very least, wipe it down with a paper towel before using.

Spicy Tofu

Break up the tofu for maximum yummy texture

Recipe on page 67

I added Doubanjiang to the usual *hiyayakko* toppings of bonito flakes, green onions and soy sauce for an energizing variation on a time-honored classic. This is even better on top of a bowl of rice.

Tofu Stir-fry

Tofu fried in sesame oil for an aroma that can't be beat

Recipe on page 67

Tofu stir-fries are best when you pair a crispy veggie with the soft tofu. I threw in some fresh sprouts and thought about what else would go well with tofu. How about some nice little dried shrimp? It turned out just as I suspected—delicious.

Sticky Tofu

A dish for people who like gooey food

Recipe on page 67

I love making cold soba noodles with a sticky topping of *natto*, okura and enoki mushrooms. I switched up the noodles for tofu and found the results to be quite tasty. The sticky condiments wrap around the slippery tofu for an easy-on-the-stomach delight.

Tofu and *Kimchi* Stew

A delectable, soul-warming stew that's super easy to make

Recipe on page 67

This is the perfect dish for cold nights when you want something warm to eat but the restaurants are all closed. The spicy *kimchi* will warm you to the bone. Try topping it off with a cup of hot sake. Perfection!

Tofu Steak
Cook slowly over low heat before flipping
Photo page 64

Ingredients
1 block silken tofu
Wheat flour, as needed
1 Tbsp butter
Dash grated garlic
1 light Tbsp soy sauce
Pepper, to taste

Instructions
1. Rinse tofu and pat dry with a paper towel, then dust top and bottom with flour.
2. Add butter to a frying pan, turn on heat and melt. Add tofu, cover with lid and cook over medium heat until both sides are browned.
3. Remove tofu, then add garlic and soy sauce to pan. Sauté briefly then pour on top of plated tofu. Sprinkle with pepper.

Note
The water in the tofu container sometimes has a strong odor, so be sure to rinse the tofu before frying.

Tofu with Chives
An added kick from freshly grated daikon
Photo page 64

Ingredients
1 block silken tofu
2" (5 cm) daikon
1/2 bundle chives
1 Tbsp soy sauce

Instructions
1. Rinse tofu and pat dry with a paper towel, then cut into bite-size pieces. Grate daikon and set aside in a colander to drain. Cut chives into small pieces.
2. Combine daikon, chives and soy sauce, then pour over plated tofu.

Tofu and Bell Pepper Salad
Simply combine with sesame oil and soy sauce
Photo page 64

Ingredients
1 block silken tofu
1 green bell pepper
2 Tbsp dried baby sardines (*jako*)
1 Tbsp sesame oil
1 Tbsp soy sauce
1 Tbsp roasted white sesame seeds

Instructions
1. Rinse tofu and pat dry with a paper towel, then dice into 1/2" (1.5 cm) cubes. Dice peppers into 2/5" (1 cm) pieces.
2. Mix all ingredients in a bowl, then serve.

Chinese-style *Hiyayakko*
Saltiness can vary widely, so be sure to taste Sichuan vegetable first
Photo page 64

Ingredients
1 block silken tofu
4" (10 cm) green onion (or leek)
Zha cai (Sichuan vegetable), to taste
1 nub ginger
1 tsp roasted white sesame seeds
1 Tbsp soy sauce
Dash oyster sauce
1 to 2 Tbsp sesame oil

Instructions
1. Rinse tofu and pat dry with a paper towel, then chop into bite-size pieces. Slice green onions into small rounds on the bias and julienne ginger. Rinse *zha cai* and finely chop.
2. Lay tofu on a dish, and pour soy sauce and oyster sauce on top, then garnish with *zha cai*, ginger, sesame seeds and green onion.
3. Heat sesame oil briefly in a small pan, then pour over tofu.

Tofu Stir-fry

Brown in a well-heated pan

Photo page 65

Ingredients

1 block silken or firm tofu
1/2 pack bean sprouts
2 *sakura* shrimp (or sub. salad shrimp)
1/2 clove garlic (minced)
1 Tbsp sesame oil
1 Tbsp sake
1 to 1 1/2 Tbsp soy sauce
Dash salt
Pepper, to taste

Instructions

1. Rinse tofu and pat dry with a paper towel.
2. In a well-heated wok, add sesame oil and garlic, then sauté over medium heat until fragrant. Add tofu and break apart with spatula while stir-frying over high heat.
3. Add sprouts and stir-fry. Add *sakura* shrimp, soy sauce, and sake. Season with salt and pepper.

Sticky Tofu

You can use noodle sauce instead of soy sauce

Photo page 65

Ingredients

1 block silken tofu
1 pack *natto* (fermented soybeans) (1 3/4 oz (50 g))
4 to 5 okra
2 to 3 enoki mushrooms (bottled or fresh)
Soy sauce, to taste

Instructions

1. Rinse tofu and pat dry with a paper towel, then cut into large pieces. Thinly slice okra into rounds.
2. Plate dish, then garnish with *natto*, okra, mushrooms and soy sauce on top.

Spicy Tofu

Lots of soy sauce and as much Doubanjiang as you like

Photo page 65

Ingredients

1 block silken tofu
1/2 green onion (or leek)
Handful bonito flakes
1 tsp Doubanjiang (Chinese chili paste)
1 Tbsp soy sauce

Instructions

1. Rinse tofu and pat dry with a paper towel, then cut into small pieces. Mince green onion.
2. In a bowl, add all ingredients and mix, breaking up tofu as you stir.

Tofu and *Kimchi* Stew

If the *kimchi* flavor is weak, add more miso

Photo page 65

Ingredients

1 block silken or firm tofu
3 1/2 oz (100 g) pork roast, thinly sliced
3 1/2 oz (100 g) Napa cabbage *kimchi*
2 tsp sesame oil
1/2 clove garlic
1/2 nub ginger
Miso and cayenne pepper, to taste

Instructions

1. Rinse tofu and pat dry with a paper towel, then cut into large pieces. Slice pork into large bite-size pieces. Mince garlic and ginger.
2. In a heated pan, add sesame oil, garlic, ginger and pork, and stir-fry.
3. Once pork is browned, add water (hot water saves time) to fill the pan 3/4 full, and bring to a boil. Skim off any foam that floats to the surface.
4. Add tofu and *kimchi* and boil briefly. Add miso gradually while checking flavor. Finish with cayenne pepper to taste.

Spicy! Spicy!

If it isn't spicy, then it's not really an appetizer! There are many intriguing spices available these days, and plenty that are still a mystery. Here I present dishes that are taken to the next level with a careful selection of easy-to-find, flavorful spices. So be brave and pile on the spice for dishes that'll make you say, "Whooooo, that's hot!"

Chicken Wings with Freshly Ground Pepper

Attack of the pepper!

Recipe on page 70

Show your guests the true power of pepper and cover that chicken in freshly ground spicy pepper. Pepper packs the biggest punch when it's freshly ground, so I suggest grinding it yourself. Go wild! Cook off the fat so the skin crisps up and is perfectly browned. That great, toothsome crunch plus a smack of spice will make you want to tear the meat right off the bone.

Chicken Wings with Freshly Ground Pepper

Work the salt and pepper into the oiled chicken

Photo page 68

Ingredients

10 chicken wings

1 tsp salt

Heaps of freshly ground pepper

1 Tbsp vegetable oil

Instructions

1. Preheat oven to 480°F (250°C).
2. Add wings to a bowl and work in salt, pepper and oil.
3. Place wings on a baking sheet and cook for 20 minutes or until golden brown.

Note

If possible, place chicken on a wire rack with water in a pan underneath. This way the chicken will cook in the steam that rises up and the fat will drip off more easily.

Kentaro's Spice Rack

You can't skimp on the spice.

First, pepper: There's nothing better than fresh-ground pepper straight from a mill. The taste is completely different from pre-ground pepper. Twist right for a helping of fine grains and left for a coarse grind. For appetizers, it's best to go big with coarse ground pepper. There are black and white peppercorns on the market, but I almost always use black, since it has a stronger taste. There are red, green and various other colors of peppercorns, too. You can use these whole for a nice visual accent in marinated or pickled dishes; they give an extra kick of spiciness. Add some pepper while making a stir-fry, then finish with even more pepper right before serving. The fresh fragrance of the pepper will waft up and make your guests salivate. It looks prettier, too.

The second category of must-have spices is chili and hot peppers. Whole dried cayenne peppers pack a mean punch. I also use plenty of chili peppers, cayenne pepper powder and seven-spice powder. If you create a strong flavor base in the dish before adding the spices, rest assured that the flavors will shine through even after adding a spicy pepper. People rarely get to cook really spicy meals, but with appetizers it's a different story. A swig of cold beer after a bite of the hot stuff is the best combination ever.

Personally, I love chili powder. It's a blend of spices that includes chilies and garlic and adds a Mexican flavor. Even people who don't like a lot of spice should try some chili powder. Even though it's called chili powder, it's not all that spicy, so I also recommend it to those who prefer milder seasonings.

I also recommend keeping spices such as mustard, Japanese *sansho* pepper, curry powder, and tabasco sauce on hand. A plate full of spice-laden appetizers is a welcome sight at any party. So spice it up!

Garlic Potato Salad

One slice of garlic per bite

Recipe on page 74

Without garlic, you just can't
make this potato salad. Cut thick
slices of garlic and fry 'em up.
Use enough garlic so you get a
nice big piece with each forkful.

Chili Beef Bits

The perfect snack

Recipe on page 74

These are like little miniature hamburgers
enhanced with loads of fragrant veggies and
spices. They're packed with flavor, so they can
be enjoyed as they are, or you can wrap them in
lettuce, or dip them into fresh salsa. These are at
their best with a cold glass of beer.

Spicy Bean and Bacon Salad

The dressing blends with the fatty bacon flavors

Recipe on page 75

Why is it always so hard to make a great bean salad at home? Maybe some recipes are missing some vital secret ingredient. There are many variations out there, but I think the safest bet is to go with a spicy concoction. Here, I use tabasco sauce.

Spicy Shrimp Sauté

Shrimp pop when mixed with spice

Recipe on page 75

This isn't your typical shrimp in chili sauce. My trick is to add some crunchy celery and a sprinkle of lemon juice. Just these two simple ingredients can create a quick Thai-style flavor. If you don't have cilantro, add celery leaves for a spot of green. Add soy sauce or *nam pla* for a truly perfect dish.

Garlic Potato Salad

Try it with a dollop of hot mustard

Photo page 72

Ingredients

1 large potato
1 to 2 cloves garlic
4 slices ham
1 Tbsp vegetable oil

A ⎰ 1 Tbsp mayonnaise
⎰ Pinch salt
⎰ Pepper, to taste
⎰ 1 tsp hot mustard
⎰ 1/2 Tbsp rice vinegar

Instructions

1. Peel potato and dice into 1 1/4" (3 cm) cubes, then soak in water for 2 to 3 minutes. In a pot, add potatoes and just enough water to cover. Boil until a skewer can be easily inserted (about 10 minutes).
2. Slice garlic cloves 1/8" (2 to 3 mm) thick. In a heated pan, add oil and garlic and sauté over low heat until garlic is crispy.
3. Slice ham into 1" (2 to 3 cm) squares.
4. In a bowl, combine mixture A, add potatoes, garlic and ham, and toss.

Chili Beef Bits

Add the celery leaves to reduce the meaty smell

Photo page 72

Ingredients

7 oz (200 g) ground beef
1/2 stalk celery, with leaves
5 red chili peppers
1 clove garlic
2 pinches salt
Pepper, to taste
Flour, as needed
Oil, for frying

Instructions

1. Finely chop celery (including leaves) and chili peppers (including seeds). Grate garlic.
2. In a bowl, combine ground beef, celery, chili peppers, garlic, salt, and pepper, and mix thoroughly.
3. Add a little oil to your hands, then form meat mixture into small logs the size of your thumb. Dust with flour.
4. In a pan, add 2/5" (1 cm) of oil and heat over medium. Add meat bits and fry, stirring occasionally, until thoroughly browned.

Spicy Bean and Bacon Salad

Balance the sturdy soybean flavor with plenty of watercress

Photo page 73

Ingredients

1 can boiled soy beans (5 1/4 oz (150 g))
3 slices bacon
Watercress, to taste
A ⎧ 1 Tbsp olive oil
⎪ 1 Tbsp rice vinegar
⎨ 2 pinches salt
⎪ Pepper, to taste
⎩ Plenty of tabasco sauce

Instructions

1. Drain soybeans. Cut bacon into 2/5" (1 cm) strips. Cut the watercress into 1/2" (1 to 2 cm) pieces.
2. In a frying pan, cook bacon over low heat until crispy.
3. In a bowl, combine mixture A. Add bacon and a small amount of rendered bacon fat, soybeans, and watercress and mix thoroughly.

Spicy Shrimp Sauté

Slice open the shrimp to turn up the volume

Photo page 73

Ingredients

10 large shrimp or prawns
1 stalk celery
Celery leaves, to taste
1 clove garlic
1 nub ginger
4 red chili peppers
1 Tbsp sesame oil
1 Tbsp rice vinegar
1 to 2 tsp soy sauce or *nam pla* (Thai fish sauce)
1 Tbsp lemon juice
Salt and pepper, to taste

Instructions

1. Shell shrimp, devein and slice open backs. Peel celery then slice thinly on the bias. Chop celery leaves. Mince garlic and ginger. Remove stem and seeds from chili peppers.
2. In a well-heated pan, add oil and sauté garlic, ginger and chili peppers over low heat.
3. Add shrimp and celery and sauté over high heat until shrimp turn opaque. Add celery leaves, soy sauce and sake, then stir to coat.
4. Stir in lemon juice and season with salt while checking flavor.

Curried Chicken and Onion

Smells great, tastes great

Recipe on page 78

Chicken and onion in a curry stew is a sure-fire hit, but I wanted to try and make a simple appetizer version. This dish has a stimulating dose of spice and fresh, juicy onions. Just add curry powder to the dressing. It's super easy. Super easy, but the flavor makes it stand out from the crowd

Honey Mustard Sweet Potatoes

A sweetness that works well with any liquor

Recipe on page 78

Fried sweet potatoes topped with a honey mayonnaise sauce is my idea of healthy junk food. This one goes great with beer or white wine. I sometimes crave something sweet like this when I'm drinking.

Spicy Sprout Sauté
The crispiness of sprouts matches nicely with the spicy seasonings

Recipe on page 79

A simple sauté that's surprisingly appetite-satisfying. I use Chinese chili paste as the main component to spice it up. Add plenty of soy sauce, since the sprouts have a hard time soaking it all up.

Sausages with Chili Powder
Succulent and juicy with a kick

Recipe on page 79

Just thinking about spiced sausages makes me salivate. Slice the sausages down the middle and let the meat juices mix in with the spices for an unbelievably tender and flavorful treat.

Potatoes with Seven-Spice Mayonnaise
Dressed-up mayonnaise has a unique flavor that's perfect for sake

Recipe on page 79

Stack potatoes, garlic, mayonnaise and seven-spice powder together and cook. The toasted mayonnaise has a unique flavor that's dense and heavy. This doesn't really go with rice, but it's perfect with alcohol.

Spicy French Fries
Use your favorite spices!

Recipe on page 79

The standard seasoning for french fries is just salt, but try adding a dash of spices to your fries for a party appetizer that'll make your guests say, "Wow!" Try using whatever spices you happen to have.

77

Curried Chicken and Onion

Season chicken with plenty of salt and pepper before frying

Photo page 76

Ingredients

1 chicken thigh (8 4/5 oz (250 g))
1 onion
1/2 Tbsp olive oil
Dash salt
Pepper, to taste

A ⎡ 1 Tbsp olive oil
⎢ 1 Tbsp rice vinegar
⎢ 2 pinches salt
⎢ Dash pepper
⎣ 1 tsp curry powder

Instructions

1. Remove fat from chicken and score thicker parts of skin and meat with a knife. Season with salt and pepper. Thinly slice onions along the grain.
2. In a well-heated pan, add oil and chicken skin-side down. Fry over high heat.
3. When chicken has browned flip over and cover. Cook over medium-low heat. Chicken is done when juices run clear.
4. Once chicken is thoroughly cooked, turn heat to high to crisp. Remove from heat and cut into 1" (2 cm) pieces.
5. In a bowl, combine mixture A and stir. Add onion, and chicken, then toss to mix.

Honey Mustard Sweet Potatoes

A mix of tangy mustard and sweet honey

Photo page 76

Ingredients

1 large sweet potato

A ⎡ 2 tsp mayonnaise
⎢ 2 tsp wholegrain mustard
⎣ 1 tsp honey

Oil, for frying

Instructions

1. Leave skin on potato and cut into 1" (2 cm) pieces.
2. In a frying pan, add oil 2/5" (1 cm) high and fry potatoes over medium heat until golden brown.
3. In a bowl, combine mixture A and potatoes, and toss to mix.

Spicy Sprout Sauté

Sauté quickly over high to keep 'em crunchy

Photo page 77

Ingredients

1 pack bean sprouts
1 clove garlic
1 nub ginger
1 Tbsp sesame oil
1 Tbsp rice vinegar
1 Tbsp soy sauce
1 tsp Doubanjiang (Chinese chili paste)
Salt and pepper, to taste

Instructions

1. Mince ginger and garlic.
2. In a well-heated wok, add sesame oil, garlic, and ginger, and stir-fry briefly. Add sprouts and sauté over high heat.
3. When sprouts turn translucent, add sake, soy sauce, and Doubanjiang, and stir-fry. Check flavor and season with salt and pepper to taste.

Potatoes with Seven-Spice Mayonnaise

You can use chili powder or even tabasco. It's up to you!

Photo page 77

Ingredients

2 potatoes
1/2 clove garlic
1 to 2 Tbsp butter
1 to 2 Tbsp mayonnaise
Seven-spice powder and salt, to taste

Instructions

1. Slice potatoes into rings 1/5" (5 mm) thick. Simmer briefly. Rub garlic onto top sides of potato slices.
2. Grease an oven-safe casserole dish with butter. Place 1 slice of potato in dish, then spread butter and mayonnaise on top, and sprinkle with seven-spice powder and salt. Add another potato slice on top and repeat process until all slices are used. Cook in toaster oven (or broiler) until golden.

Sausages with Chili Powder

Try combining different kinds of sausages

Photo page 77

Ingredients

10 large sausage links
1 tsp chili powder
1 tsp olive oil

Instructions

1. Slice open sausages lengthwise, then baste lightly with oil. Lay on toaster oven pan and sprinkle with chili powder.
2. Cook in toaster oven for 5 minutes, or until sliced part of sausages puff up.

Spicy French Fries

The trick is to fry the fries over low heat until they're nice and fluffy

Photo page 77

Ingredients

5 1/4 oz (150 g) frozen french fries
Salt, to taste
Spice mix: dash each pepper, onion powder, paprika, turmeric, curry powder, etc.
Oil, for frying

Instructions

1. In a pan, add 2/5" (1 cm) oil, add frozen fries, then turn on heat. Fry over medium heat until golden brown.
2. Remove from heat and sprinkle with spice mix and salt while still hot. Stir.

Fried Potatoes and Pickled *Takana*

The *takana* adds a salty depth

Recipe on page 82

Mash the potatoes in the pan as you fry them. Crumble the *mentaiko* and toss it in, making sure to distribute roe throughout the potatoes evenly. One day I happened to have extra pickled *takana* in the fridge and added it in, just for kicks. It turned out even better than I'd imagined.

Fast Frying Pan Favorites

It can be fun making appetizers on a whim, when you have a sudden craving, or when one of your guests comes up with a special request. You can continue the conversation, wine glass still in hand, as you whip up exquisite dishes with equal care and delight. My favorite part is hearing how much everyone enjoyed them—that's just the best kind of reward.

Two-Way Fritters

A surprisingly delightful crunch

Recipe on page 83

One has onions and *sakura* shrimp, and the other contains corn, ham and edamame—two great fritters fried slowly over low heat. These are crispy snacks that can top any appetizer best-of list. Since you fry them slowly, it takes some time, but that's okay. You can always relax with a beer or hum away to your heart's content.

Fried Potatoes and Pickled *Takana*

When the potatoes are browned, flavor with a bit of soy sauce

Photo page 80

Ingredients

2 potatoes
3 oz (80 g) pickled *takana* (mustard greens)
1/2 sac *mentaiko* (pollock roe)
1/2 clove garlic
1 Tbsp roasted white sesame seeds
Pinch salt
Dash soy sauce
1 Tbsp sesame oil

Instructions

1. Peel potatoes and cut into small pieces and soak in water for 2 to 3 minutes. Finely chop *takana*. Remove membrane from *mentaiko* and crumble. Mince garlic.
2. In a pot, add potatoes and just enough water to cover. Cover with a lid and boil for 10 minutes (or until tender), then drain in a colander.
3. In a frying pan, heat oil and sauté garlic over medium heat.
4. Add potatoes to pan and lightly mash while stir-frying. Once potatoes are browned, stir in *takana*.
5. Add soy sauce, salt and sesame seeds. Add *mentaiko* last and stir-fry briefly.

Note

1 sac of *mentaiko* contains 2 pieces.

Two-Way Fritters

Cook over low heat—
they stay crispy even when cooled

Photo page 81

Ingredients

A
- 1 can corn (5 1/4 oz (150 g))
- 5 slices ham
- 1/2 C frozen shelled edamame

B
- 2 stalks green onion (or leek)
- 3 Tbsp *sakura* (or salad) shrimp

C
- 1 C wheat flour
- 2/5 C water
- Pinch salt

Instructions

1. Combine mixture C and divide between two bowls.
2. Slice ham into 1" (2 cm) squares. Rinse edamame in water to thaw. In one of the bowls with batter, add mixture A and stir to coat.
3. Slice green onions from mixture B into small pieces, then add to other bowl of batter. Add shrimp to bowl and stir to coat.
4. The cooking process is the same for both fritters: Add oil to a pan and heat over medium-low heat. Scoop fritters out of bowls with a spatula and carefully place in oil. Fry over low heat until fritters are crispy and golden. Remove from oil, drain, sprinkle with salt and serve.

Note
You can also use fava beans instead of edamame.

Clams in Oyster Sauce

Shell-on for a lovely presentation

Recipe on page 86

Stir-fry these clams with the shells on. Pick them up one at a time and slurp down the meat along with that tasty, thick sauce. Sake lovers will be totally thrilled with this appetizer.

Potatoes and Bacon in Cream Sauce

Succulent bacon

Recipe on page 86

If you can, get thickly sliced bacon from the deli counter or butcher. The sauce is a lot like carbonara. I'm a huge fan of carbonara sauce.

Fried *Konnyaku*
Fragrant soy sauce
Recipe on page 87

When the *konnyaku* starts popping and snapping in the frying pan, for some reason I imagine that I can smell the tempting scent of soy sauce wafting up. But I don't actually add any soy sauce until after the *konnyaku* is nice and browned. Weird, right?

Chikuwa in Peanut Sauce
Peanut sauce is a sure-fire hit!
Recipe on page 87

Maybe it's just me, but *chikuwa* always makes me think of street food. That's why I feel that a rich sauce is the best way to dress it up. This dish has a flavor that will bring you back to summer nights and street vendors.

Fried Garlic
Light, fluffy and smooth inside
Recipe on page 87

It's so easy. No batter, no seasoning—it's not your typical batter-fried fare. Just fry the whole clove, skin and all. It'll puff up all nice and crispy on the outside.

Garlic Sprout Stir-fry
You can't lose with a crunch like this
Recipe on page 87

If you don't cook the sprouts just right they'll be mushy or rubbery, so be sure to stir-fry 'em over high heat. *Sakura* shrimp are the perfect counterpoint in this dish.

Clams in Oyster Sauce

The oyster sauce is rich and flavorful and pepper adds a fragrant layer

Photo page 84

Ingredients

7 oz (200 g) clams (shell on, soaked to remove sand)
1 clove garlic
2 Tbsp sake
1 to 2 tsp oyster sauce
1 tsp soy sauce
Pepper, to taste
1 Tbsp sesame oil

Instructions

1. Halve garlic lengthwise and remove any green cores. Mash with the flat of a knife.
2. In a pan, add sesame oil and garlic and sauté over medium-low heat.
3. When garlic is browned, add clams and turn heat to high.
4. Add sake and stir-fry. When clam shells open, add oyster sauce, soy sauce and pepper and stir to coat.

Potatoes and Bacon in Cream Sauce

Cook the bacon 'til it's crisp

Photo page 84

Ingredients

3 potatoes
1 slice bacon 2/5" (1 cm) thick
1 clove garlic
1/2 Tbsp butter
2/5 C (100 ml) fresh cream
2 Tbsp powdered Parmesan cheese
Dash salt
Pepper, to taste

Instructions

1. Peel potatoes and slice each into about six chunks. Soak in water for 2 to 3 minutes. Add potatoes to a pot, cover with just enough water, then boil for 10 minutes (or until a skewer can be inserted).
2. Cut bacon into 1" (2 cm) pieces. Mince garlic.
3. Add butter to frying pan and turn on heat. Add bacon and cook over high, blotting rendered fat with a paper towel.
4. When bacon is crisp, add garlic and fry until golden brown. Add fresh cream and stir briefly.
5. Add Parmesan cheese and simmer. Check flavor and season with salt and pepper. When sauce has thickened, add potatoes and stir-fry until evenly coated. Plate and finish with pepper.

Note
Cut the potatoes into big pieces. The sauce is rich, so big slices hold up better than smaller ones. Be sure to use real cream, too.

Fried *Konnyaku*

Use high heat the whole time

Photo page 85

Ingredients

1 block plain *konnyaku* (konjac jelly)
1 Tbsp sesame oil
1/2 Tbsp sake
1 Tbsp soy sauce
Dash grated garlic
Seven-spice powder, to taste

Instructions

1. Rinse *konnyaku* and cut into 1" (2 cm) pieces. Place *konnyaku* in a colander, and douse with plenty of hot water.
2. In a well-heated pan, add sesame oil and *konnyaku* and sauté over high heat.
3. When the surface of *konnyaku* toughens up, add sake and soy sauce, then stir to coat. Remove from heat and stir in grated garlic.
4. Plate and finish with seven-spice powder.

Fried Garlic

Add garlic to warm oil and fry on medium-low

Photo page 85

Ingredients

7 to 8 cloves garlic
Salt and pepper, to taste
Oil, for frying

Instructions

1. In a pan, add 2/5" (1 cm) oil and heat over low.
2. Add unpeeled, separated garlic cloves to oil and fry over medium-low until lightly browned, or until a skewer can be easily inserted. Remove from oil and drain on a wire rack. Season with salt and pepper.

Chikuwa in Peanut Sauce

Butter adds depth to the flavor

Photo page 85

Ingredients

3 *chikuwa* (tube-shaped fish cake. Or sub. surimi)
2 to 3 Tbsp buttered peanuts
1/2 Tbsp butter
1 tsp Worcestershire sauce
Pepper and dried seaweed (*aonori*), to taste

Instructions

1. Slice *chikuwa* into rings 2/5" (1 cm) thick.
2. In a pan, add butter and turn on heat. Add *chikuwa* and stir-fry over high heat until browned. Add peanuts.
3. When peanuts are browned, add Worcestershire sauce and stir-fry. Season with pepper and stir.
4. Serve on dish and finish with dried seaweed.

Garlic Sprout Stir-fry

Try scallops instead of shrimp if you like

Photo page 85

Ingredients

2 bunches garlic sprouts
1 Tbsp *sakura* (or salad) shrimp
1 nub ginger
1 Tbsp sesame oil
1 Tbsp sake
1/2 to 1 Tbsp soy sauce
Dash each salt and pepper

Instructions

1. Cut sprouts into 2" (5 cm) pieces. Mince ginger.
2. In a pan, heat oil and add garlic sprouts and minced ginger. Sauté over high heat.
3. When sprouts are tender, add salt, pepper and sake, then shrimp. Stir-fry, then add soy sauce and stir to coat.

Uni Potatoes
Add lots of sauce!

Recipe on page 90

Smash up those sea urchins with gusto to create this decadent sauce. You might probably think it's wasteful to use fresh *uni* in a dressing. In this recipe I use bottled sea urchin and mix it with fresh cream.

Whelk Sauté
Rich and very flavorful

Recipe on page 90

Mushroom and Garlic Sauté
Use a mix of mushrooms

Recipe on page 90

Whelks, or sea snails, are cheap, and more importantly, they're delicious. What more could you ask for? Add grated garlic and onion for a great dish that your guests would happily hand over money for.

There are so many types of mushrooms, each with a distinct flavor. Use mushrooms that are in season, since their flavors are at their best. Sauté the mushrooms in oil that's been infused with garlic and chili peppers. You'll be hooked on mushrooms in no time.

Napa Cabbage Miso Sauté
Just Napa cabbage and a mouthful of spice

Recipe on page 91

Choose a small head of cabbage and use just one-fourth. It might seem like a lot, especially for a small gathering, but when served up with miso, it'll be gone before you know it. This is a super-quick dish—just season and set aside.

Chicken Gizzard Sauté

A divine, toothsome delicacy

Recipe on page 91

Gizzards might sound intimidating, but their preparation is really simple. They're inexpensive, don't need a whole lot of prep work and have a unique texture and flavor. Truly, a great choice for an appealing appetizer.

Wood Ear Mushroom Scramble

Fluffy eggs and savory mushrooms

Recipe on page 91

This is also a very cheap dish. Add whisked eggs and let them cook undisturbed for a while, then turn over with a wooden spatula to mix. Add onions and garlic for a slightly Oriental flavor.

Uni Potatoes

The saltiness of the sea urchin is subdued by the thick cream

Photo page 88

Ingredients

1 potato
2 tsp mashed *uni* (sea urchin) (bottled)
1 tsp vegetable oil
1 Tbsp butter
1/5 C (50 cc) fresh cream
Dash chives

Instructions

1. Peel potato and cut into rounds 2/5" (1 cm) thick. Soak in water for 2 to 3 minutes, then pat dry. Cut chives into small pieces.
2. In a heated pan, add oil. Add potato slices side by side and cook over low heat, covered, until a skewer can be easily inserted. Turn heat to high and brown both sides of potatoes.
3. In a small pot, melt butter over low heat. Add *uni* and cook over low heat. Stir until evenly mixed, then add cream and cook until mixture bubbles.
4. Serve potatoes on a dish, pour *uni* sauce on top and garnish with sliced chives.

Mushroom and Garlic Sauté

Cook over low heat for a spicy, garlic-y flavor

Photo page 88

Ingredients

1 pack shimeji mushrooms
1 pack maitake (sheep's head) mushrooms
2 to 3 shiitake mushrooms
1 clove garlic
1 chili pepper, deseeded
1 Tbsp olive oil
1/2 tsp soy sauce
2 pinches salt
Pepper, to taste

Instructions

1. Slice off tough root ends of shimeji and maitake mushrooms, then break into small clusters. Remove stems from shiitake mushrooms then slice into large pieces. Mince garlic.
2. In a pan, add oil, salt, garlic and chili pepper, then sauté over low heat.
3. Add all mushrooms and turn heat to high. When mushrooms are tender, add soy sauce and pepper. Stir to mix, then remove from heat.

Note
If you don't use enough salt and pepper, it'll taste bland. Taste before serving and adjust seasoning as needed.

Whelk Sauté

After seasoning, don't sauté for too much longer

Photo page 88

Ingredients

5 1/4 oz (150 g) boiled whelks
A ⎰ 2 Tbsp grated onion
⎱ 1/2 clove garlic, grated
⎱ 1 light Tbsp soy sauce
1 Tbsp butter
Dash salt
Pepper, to taste

Instructions

1. In a pan, add butter then turn on heat. Add whelks and sauté over medium heat.
2. When the whelks are cooked through, add mixture A and stir-fry. Season with salt and pepper.

Note
After adding seasonings, allow flavors to absorb briefly, then remove from heat. If the onions cook for too long they'll lose their delicate flavor.

Napa Cabbage Miso Sauté

Simply sauté over high heat

Photo page 88

Ingredients

1/4 head Napa cabbage

A
- 1 Tbsp miso
- 1 Tbsp sake
- 1 Tbsp mirin (sweet cooking wine)
- 1/2 clove garlic, grated

1 Tbsp sesame oil

Dash salt

Pepper and cayenne pepper, to taste

Instructions

1. Separate cabbage into leaves and stems. Chop the leaves into 2" (5 cm) chunks and julienne stems. In a bowl, combine mixture A.
2. In a heated wok, add oil and stems of cabbage, then sauté over medium.
3. Add cabbage leaves, then salt and pepper. When the cabbage is tender add mixture A and cook over high heat.
4. Serve on a dish and finish with cayenne pepper.

Chicken Gizzard Sauté

Use heaps of green onions

Photo page 89

Ingredients

7 oz (200 g) chicken gizzard

3 green onions (or leeks)

1/2 clove garlic

1/2 nub ginger

1 Tbsp sesame oil

1 to 2 Tbsp sake

1 tsp soy sauce

Instructions

1. Chop green onions into fine rounds. Mince garlic and ginger.
2. In a well-heated pan, add oil, garlic and ginger then sauté over medium heat until fragrant. Add gizzards and sauté thoroughly.
3. Add sake and soy sauce, then stir-fry over high heat. Add green onions and briefly stir.

Note

This dish works best when the green onions retain their spiciness, so add them last. If cooked too long, the onions will turn sweet.

Wood Ear Mushroom Scramble

The base is salt, the hidden flavor is soy sauce

Photo page 89

Ingredients

3 1/2 oz (100 g) thinly sliced pork

2 Tbsp dried wood ear mushroom

2 eggs

1 green onion (or leek)

1/2 clove garlic

1 Tbsp sesame oil

2 pinch salt

Pepper, to taste

Instructions

1. Reconstitute mushrooms in water. Thinly chop onion and garlic.
2. In a well-heated wok, add oil, green onion, garlic and pork, then sauté over medium heat. Add mushrooms and sprinkle lightly with salt.
3. When the pork is cooked, add whisked eggs. When the eggs begin to solidify, stir with wide strokes. When eggs are done, season with salt and pepper.

Grand Finale: Rice Dishes

You can't end a food-fueled party without a rice dish capper. That being said, it doesn't have to be a massive, donburi-size meal. With soup-based dishes and *ochazuke*, you really don't want to overload on the rice. Keep it small and simple. If the appetizers have been light and fresh, serve a rice dish that's just a little heavier. Adding bonito flakes and soy sauce is a simple way to flavor rice, but it's the perfect way to end a night of drinking.

Rice with Bonito Flakes

Serve it up in a pretty bowl

Recipe on page 94

My friends always love this one. Re-done rice isn't something you'll find in restaurants, but that doesn't mean it's not yummy. Make sure you pile on the toppings. If you serve it in a really nice dish, it makes it seem that much more luxurious.

Garlic Rice
Garlic is all you need
Recipe on page 94

Garlic sure is special, isn't it?
But you have to get the hang
of sautéing it just right. Add
the garlic and oil before you
turn on the heat, and sauté
over low until golden. You
can't go wrong.

Grilled Fish
Ochazuke
Roasted tea and dried mackerel
Recipe on page 95

Houjicha, or roasted
tea, is a perfect
match for dried
mackerel. The dried
fish is plenty salty
all on its own, but
you might want to
sprinkle some extra
salt on top to
heighten the flavors.

Fried Rice Patties
Majorly satisfying with just a little rice
Recipe on page 95

Try this recipe when you only
have a little rice left over. Just
one regular serving of rice turns
into four servings of this pan-fried
treat. Add whatever leftovers you
have to pump up the flavor—
onions, baby sardines, or maybe
even ham and cheese.

Chicken and Rice Soup
A definite winner
Recipe on page 95

This super easy, super tasty
soup is ready in 15 minutes flat.
Boil the chicken wings, shred
the meat off the bones, and add
it on top of the rice. Pour in the
soup and voilà! It's done.

Rice with Bonito Flakes

Add plenty of bonito flakes

Photo page 92

Ingredients (serves 2)

2 servings rice
Bonito flakes (*katsuobushi*), as desired
Scallions, grilled seaweed (*yakinori*) and soy sauce,
   to taste

Instructions

1. Chop scallions and tear seaweed into bite-size pieces.
2. Serve rice in bowls. Add bonito flakes, scallions and seaweed on top of rice and sprinkle with a dash of soy sauce.

Garlic Rice

Once the garlic has flavored the oil, remove from the frying pan

Photo page 93

Ingredients (serves 2)

2 servings rice
4 cloves garlic
1 Tbsp vegetable oil
1 tsp butter
2 pinches salt
Pepper, to taste
1/2 tsp soy sauce
Parsley (fresh, if possible), to taste

Instructions

1. Cut garlic into very thin (1 to 2 mm) slices. Finely chop parsley.
2. In a pan, add oil and garlic and sauté slowly over low heat until golden and crispy. Remove from pan.
3. Add rice to pan and break up any clumps while sautéing over medium heat.
4. Return garlic to pan. Add butter, salt and pepper, then mix into rice. Sprinkle with soy sauce.
5. Serve in dishes and garnish with parsley.

Grilled Fish *Ochazuke*

Use small portions of rice

Photo page 93

Ingredients (serves 2)

2 small servings rice
2 pieces dried mackerel
Dash salt
Roasted green tea (*houjicha*) and scallions, to taste

Instructions

1. Preheat oven to 480°F (250°C). Add water to a pan. Place mackerel on a wire rack, then place over pan with water. Cook in oven for 15 minutes. Remove from oven and shred meat from bones. Brew tea.
2. Add rice to bowls and place shredded mackerel on top. Sprinkle with salt. Cut scallions into 1 1/4" (3 cm) pieces and garnish. Pour hot tea over rice before serving.

Fried Rice Patties

Make thin patties and fry over low heat

Photo page 93

Ingredients (yields 4)

1 serving cooked rice
1 egg
1 Tbsp red pickled ginger, julienned
Scallions, to taste
2 Tbsp dried baby sardines (*chirimen jako*)
2 Tbsp flour
1 Tbsp water
Dash salt
Sesame oil and soy sauce, to taste

Chicken and Rice Soup

Accent with ginger—or try adding black pepper

Photo page 93

Ingredients (yields 4 servings)

4 servings cooked rice
4 chicken wings
Soup ⎡ 1 green onion (or leek), green part
⎢ 1/2 clove garlic
⎢ 1 nub ginger
⎢ 3 1/2 C warm water
⎣ Dash each soy sauce and salt
White part of green onion from above, finely chopped
Grated ginger, to taste
Sesame oil, roasted white sesame seeds, *mitsuba* (or watercress), as desired

Instructions

1. Make soup: Bring water to a boil in a pot. Add chicken wings, green part of green onion, garlic and ginger, then boil for 15 minutes over medium heat. Skim off any foam that floats to the surface.
2. Strain soup and take out chicken. Remove skin and bones from chicken, shred meat and set aside to cool. Reheat soup in pot and season with salt and soy sauce.
3. Add rice to bowls. Place shredded chicken meat on top and garnish with white part of green onion, ginger, sesame oil, sesame seeds and *mitsuba*. Pour soup over rice.

Note

The main seasoning for this soup is salt. Season with salt and add soy sauce for a fragrant top note.

Instructions

1. Chop scallions into small rounds.
2. Add all ingredients except sesame oil and soy sauce to a bowl. Mix well.
3. In a heated pan, add sesame oil. Pour in mixture from step 2 into a circle and cook, covered, over low heat. Flip and fry until both sides are lightly browned.
4. Baste with soy sauce on each side and fry until crispy.

Kentaro Kobayashi

Born 1972 in Tokyo, Japan. Kentaro began working as an illustrator while attending the Musashino College of Fine Arts, and simultaneously put his inborn love of cooking to work by becoming a culinary artist. In addition to charismatically introducing recipes on television and in magazines, he helped develop ready-made recipes for retail sale and also hosted cooking classes, among other various activities. Kentaro's motto is "Easy and delicious, stylish yet realistic." In particular he proposes menus and meal plans based on what he himself wants to eat and make, in keeping with his lifestyle and the idea of always being practical. This book is written from that perspective and draws on the author's own personal experience.

Appetizer Rex

Translation: Jessica Bezer
Vetting: Glory Gallo

Copyright © 2009 by Kentaro Kobayashi
Photography © 2009 by Hideo Sawai

Published by Vertical, Inc., New York.

Originally published in Japanese as *Dokanto, Umai Tsumami* by Bunka Shuppankyoku, Tokyo, 1999.

ISBN 978-1-934287-63-7

Manufactured in The United States of America

First American Edition

Vertical, Inc.
www.vertical-inc.com